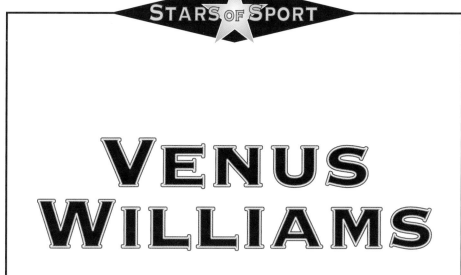

VENUS WILLIAMS

BY **P.M. BOEKHOFF**
AND **STUART A. KALLEN**

KIDHAVEN PRESS™

THOMSON
™
GALE

San Diego • Detroit • New York • San Francisco • Cleveland
New Haven, Conn. • Waterville, Maine • London • Munich

THOMSON
GALE

© 2003 by KidHaven Press. KidHaven Press is an imprint of The Gale Group, Inc.,
a division of Thomson Learning, Inc.

KidHaven™ and Thomson Learning™ are trademarks used herein under license.

For more information, contact
KidHaven Press
27500 Drake Rd.
Farmington Hills, MI 48331-3535
Or you can visit our Internet site at http://www.gale.com

LIBRARY OF CONGRESS CATALOGING-IN-PUBLICATION DATA

Boekhoff, P.M. (Patti Marlene), 1957–
 Venus Williams / by P.M. Boekhoff & Stuart A. Kallen.
 p. cm.—(Stars of sport)
Summary: Discusses the childhood, family, and tennis career of Venus Williams.
Includes bibliographical references (p.   ) and index.
 ISBN 0-7377-1395-X (alk. paper)
1. Williams, Venus, 1980—Juvenile literature. 2. Tennis players—United States—
Biography—Juvenile literature. 3. African American women tennis players—
Biography—Juvenile literature. I. Kallen, Stuart A., 1955– II. Title. III. Series.
 GV994.W994 B64 2003
 796.342'092—dc21

                                                                2002008578

Printed in the United States of America.

Contents

Tennis Lessons

Venus Williams is one of the best tennis players in the sport's history. She revolutionized tennis and brought excitement, new fans, and a great sense of style to the sport.

Williams began playing when she was little more than four years old. By 2002 she was ranked number one in the world among female tennis professionals. Along with her sister Serena, Venus Williams is one of the few African Americans playing a sport historically dominated by European and European American players. As a result, while striving to become the world's greatest female tennis star, Venus Williams has also had to deal with issues of racial prejudice. But Venus believed in herself, and she proved to the world that she was the very best.

Venus Ebone Starr Williams was born on June 17, 1980, in Lynwood, California, a suburb of Los Angeles. Her younger sister Serena was born a little more than a year later, on September 26. Venus and Serena have three older sisters: Yetunde, Isha, and Lyndrea.

Even before Venus and Serena were born, their father Richard Dove Williams decided he would teach them to be tennis champions. However, Mr. Williams was not a professional tennis coach. Instead, he ran a private security business. His wife Oracene was a nurse.

Mr. Williams wanted his whole family to play tennis. So he studied books, magazines, and videos to

Venus Williams lunges toward the ball for a powerful return at the 2002 French Open.

learn about the sport. The family moved to the Compton neighborhood in Los Angeles, where the three oldest girls practiced on public tennis courts. Mrs. Williams also played tennis twice a day, before and after work—even when she was pregnant with Venus. As Mr. Williams gained experience coaching his fam-

After a tennis lesson, Venus's father playfully pushes her around the court in a shopping cart.

ily, he decided to teach others as well, and soon became a neighborhood tennis coach.

The Compton Courts

When Venus was four years old, her father took her to the park for her first tennis lessons. He brought along six tennis rackets and seven milk crates full of old, worn-out tennis balls. There were only two courts in Compton, and they were made of old, slippery asphalt, with weeds growing up through the cracks. Standing on those crumbling courts, Mr. Williams told his little daughter that someday she would be one of the best tennis players in the world. He later said:

> The first time I knew Venus was going to be a good tennis player was the first time I took her out on her very first day. I was working with some other kids, and had a shopping cart that would hold 550 balls. It took three kids who were teenagers a long time to hit those balls. They wanted to take breaks. Well, while they were taking a break, Venus wanted to hit every ball in that basket. She wouldn't stop. Every time you tried to stop her, she would start crying.[1]

In 1985 Serena joined Venus in the tennis lessons with their father. Although the playing was fun, the neighborhood where the courts were located was one of the most dangerous in the United States. The Williams sisters later remembered ducking gunfire while they were practicing. But nearby gang members

A young Venus Williams leans on a wall covered by graffiti in Compton where she began playing tennis.

came to know them and offered them protection when the shooting started. In this environment the girls conquered their fears, learned quickly, and developed very advanced playing skills at an early age.

Confidence and Determination

By the time she was eight years old, Venus demonstrated her talents to some of the best players in the

Los Angeles area. In 1988 tennis stars John McEnroe and Pete Sampras watched Venus play with professional tennis teacher Paul Cohen at a private court in Brentwood. Later, both stars played tennis with Venus. Mr. Williams told Venus that McEnroe took it easy on her, but she did not believe him. She told her father that she thought she could have won the match.

The next year, Venus and Serena played in their first tennis **tournament**. They both won all their games and ended up playing against one another in the final championship. Venus beat Serena, and those who watched were amazed to see two sisters competing so strongly against each other. The Williams sisters continued to enter tournaments in the influential junior tennis circuit, competing with other young players and winning almost all the time.

Venus and Serena were among the few players on the junior circuit who had come from an inner-city neighborhood. The parents of most of the other young players had spent tens of thousands of dollars for lessons at exclusive tennis clubs and travel to tournaments. Some of these people were mean to Venus, and her father became so disgusted with them that he tried to make her quit tennis. But Venus loved it so much that she would not give it up.

Venus Has Many Talents

When she was ten years old, Venus started to attract the attention of sports reporters. The *New York Times* ran articles about her great future as a tennis player.

Don King raises the peace sign. Venus turned down a contract with the famous promoter in 1991.

But in a front-page story, Venus told *Times* reporters she wanted to be an astronaut instead!

Venus's parents did not like the attention from reporters. They wanted to protect her so she could enjoy a normal childhood. The reporters continued to follow Venus, however, and she had to change elementary schools three times to avoid them. And in addition to the glowing news coverage, Venus was showered with gifts of clothing, shoes, and tennis gear by companies who wanted to give her large sums of money to **endorse**, or support, their products. This sparked Venus's interest in fashion design, and she began to use her old clothing to create stylish clothes for her dolls.

Venus Meets the Pros

Coaches from all over the world invited Venus to their private tennis camps. Agents offered her family houses, cars, and millions of dollars for the right to represent her. For example, in May 1991, sports promoter Don King came to Compton in a limo. He took the Williams family to lunch to talk about managing the two young players. In July the sisters wore white polo shirts with the King Productions logo on the sleeves while playing in the Southern California Tennis Association sectional championships. However, they did not sign with the promoter.

Both *Sports Illustrated* and *Tennis* magazine noticed Venus's talent and ran stories on her in the summer of 1991. That year, her father invited tennis teaching pro Ric Macci to come to Compton to watch the girls play. Macci played a few games with Venus but was not impressed at first. After the game, however, Venus got Macci's attention when she walked on her hands for a distance of thirty feet and then did backward cartwheels for another thirty feet. The coach was very impressed when he saw that the eleven-year-old girl still had plenty of energy left after playing him.

Venus Stays in School

Venus and Serena continued to play in national junior tennis tournaments, the only path to stardom for

Venus receives instructions from her father, Richard (far right), and coach Ric Macci.

young tennis players. In September 1991, Venus was ranked number one among southern California girls twelve and under, and Serena was ranked number one in the ten-and-under division. Venus had won an impressive sixty-three games in a row, and had lost none.

Richard Williams pulled his daughters out of junior tennis and enrolled them in Ric Macci's Delray Beach, Florida, tennis academy. Macci got a clothing endorsement deal for the sisters, which financed the family's move to a twenty-one acre estate in nearby Palm Beach Gardens, Florida. After the family moved to

Florida, Macci coached the sisters six hours a day, six days a week.

While other young, talented tennis players traveled and competed in tournaments, Venus stayed home, studied, and became an A student. Although she loved tennis, education was her first priority.

Venus and her sister Serena enjoy spending time together on the court.

Venus's parents (seen here with her in 1994) taught her the importance of a good education.

Venus also found time in her busy schedule to visit schools to talk with children about sports and the importance of a good education. Even though she was still very young herself, Venus began to give her time to help others.

Chapter Two

Young Professional

Venus Williams was a major tennis star by the time she was eleven years old. When she reached fourteen, she was old enough to play in professional tournaments. Many athletes who become pros at such an early age have short careers because the pressure to perform is so hard. They drop out of school to make huge amounts of money, and some get into trouble and lose their joy for the game. But because Venus made good grades, her father let her go on to become a professional player.

In October, one week before Venus played her first pro game, the pressure started. The family's legal advisor suggested that Venus sign a tennis shoe endorsement deal before the match. He argued that if her first

Venus, age ten, playfully poses in a pile of tennis balls.

game were a disaster, she might lose the deal. Then Coach Macci called to suggest that Venus practice more. Not wanting his daughter to feel the pressure, Richard Williams decided to take the family on a one-week trip to Disney World instead.

Betting on Venus

Mr. Williams was betting that Venus was ready to be a great success. He was also sure that offers would come if she won her first professional game. At the Bank of the West Classic in Oakland on October 31, Venus proved him right. She caused a sensation by defeating Shaun Stafford, who was ranked number fifty-nine. This meant that Venus beat the fifty-ninth best player in the world.

In her next match of the tournament, Venus faced Arantxa Sanchez Vicario, the number two player in the world. Venus started out in the lead and played very well. But Sanchez Vicario, who was a much more experienced player, eventually won the game. In an interview after the tournament, Venus was asked to compare her loss to other losses in her past. She answered dreamily that she had never lost a tennis match before.

Venus performed brilliantly in her first tournament. As soon as the match was over, offers came in from several tennis shoe companies. On May 22, 1995, Venus signed a five-year, $12 million deal with Reebok to endorse its products.

Venus in Style

As a professional, Venus was allowed to play in as many tournaments as she wished, but she stayed in school and played only a few competitions. When she lost in the first round in a tournament in August 1995, some tennis experts said that she had not learned to compete properly while touring in the junior tennis circuit. Because Venus had learned her game mostly by playing against her sister Serena, she had little experience playing against others.

Venus lost matches, but she learned to play against her new opponents. She became known for her unique style of play—and for her unique hairstyle as well. On the tennis court, Venus often wore eighteen hundred pearly beads in her hair, a hairdo that took ten hours

Venus sports her unique beaded hairdo at Wimbledon in 1998.

to complete. For the next three years Venus wore the beads on courts all over the world, sometimes giving them to adoring fans when they fell out.

Some players did not like the sound of the beads clicking against each other as she played. But her many fans found her sense of style as inspiring as her powerful, determined grace on the court. And wherever tennis was played, even in fashionable France, young girls imitated her braided and beaded hairstyle.

Wimbledon

Venus played at Wimbledon, England, for the first time on June 28, 1997. Wimbledon is one of the most important tennis tournaments in the world. Along with the U.S. Open, the Australian Open, and the French Open, Wimbledon is one of the tournaments in tennis's **Grand Slam**. At first Venus played well at Wimbledon, where the grass surface was good for her fast, aggressive style of play. But she soon lost to Magdalena Grzybowska of Poland, who was ranked number ninety-one. At one point, Venus went ahead with a serve even though she had a broken racket string. Critics said that as she continued to play, Venus seemed to have lost her desire to score points.

Headlines in newspapers around the world the next day read "VENUS OUT OF ORBIT!" and "VENUS HAS TUMBLED BACK TO EARTH."[2] But Venus believed in herself, and she did not seem to be bothered by others' lack of faith in her. She simply said, "It's my first Wimbledon. There will be many more."[3]

Althea Gibson reaches for a return at Wimbledon in 1956.

Tennis and Prejudice at the U.S. Open

Three months later, on September 7, 1997, Venus played in the U.S. Open, winning six games but losing the final (seventh) game. This was an important milestone in her life—the seventeen-year-old Williams was the first African American woman since Althea Gibson to reach the finals in the U.S. Open. Gibson had won the tournament in 1957 and in 1958.

This was a special time and place for Williams to achieve this goal—the stadium was named after African American tennis star Arthur Ashe, and the tournament began on Althea Gibson's seventieth birthday. Gibson and Ashe had both broken racial barriers that kept African Americans out of the game for many years. It seemed like a great time for harmony between players. But several players tried to distract Venus with racist remarks, then complained publicly about her not smiling at them or being friendly to them. Reporters then swarmed around Williams, asking her

The stadium where Venus Williams played in the U.S. Open was named after Arthur Ashe, seen here winning at Wimbledon in 1968.

Thousands of excited fans watch the opening ceremony of the U.S. Open at Arthur Ashe Stadium, where Venus won six of seven games in 1997.

about the negativity and racism instead of asking about her tennis game.

Venus was able to gather strength from the words of her mother, who had taught her at an early age not to take criticism personally. Venus graciously turned their attention to the positive when she said, "I think with this moment in the first year in Arthur Ashe Stadium, it all represents everyone being together, everyone having a chance to play. So I think this is definitely ruining the mood, these questions about racism."[4]

In the final game of the tournament, Williams lost the championship to the number one player in the world, Martina Hingis. But Williams played so well that her ranking moved from number sixty-six to number twenty-seven in one day. People who knew the game predicted that Venus would become a great player. The bright young star was full of grace, both on the court and off.

A Well-Rounded Young Woman

Williams was also one of the most intelligent players. When she traveled across the world to play in tournaments, she learned the history, art, and languages of the countries she visited. And she continued with her studies at school as well, graduating in January 1998 from Driftwood Academy High School with an A average.

In her teenage years, Venus Williams had become a worldwide tennis sensation. While she remained focused on her game, she also took time to become an educated and eloquent young woman. And in doing so, she became a respected role model for millions of young people around the world.

Chapter Three

The Sisters

Venus and Serena played together and studied together. When Venus decided to go to college to study fashion design, Serena enrolled, too. Venus had been interested in fashion design since her childhood, and, at the age of eighteen, she designed seven dresses of different colors to wear at the U.S. Open.

Venus wore a different dress at each match. And one of the outfits, a red, white, and blue dress, was made to be worn for the final match. Venus lost the **semifinals**, however, to Lindsay Davenport, so she did not get to wear the dress. Venus later said: "I'm deeply saddened that I didn't have the opportunity to wear my seventh dress. I'm actually going to put that one in a coffin and bury it."[5]

Serena Williams jokes with the media at the 1999 U.S. Open. Serena beat Venus for the first time later that year.

In addition to clothing design, Venus was interested in writing poetry and prose. In December 1998, Venus and Serena together used their writing skills to design and publish their own newsletter, "The Tennis Monthly Recap." They distributed the newsletter at the Australian Open the following month. For their first issue, they interviewed their hero, Pete Sampras, and Venus wrote an article praising her sister Serena.

Serena's Biggest Competition

Although the two sisters were able to cooperate on their newsletter, they had to compete against each other more often on the tennis court. This caused great stress within the family, so in 1999 the Williams sisters decided not to enter the same events.

While avoiding competition with each other, the sisters continued to dominate the sport. On February 28, 1999, Venus won a title in Oklahoma City on the same day that Serena won the Paris Indoors. With this feat, the Williams sisters became the first sisters in professional tennis history to each win a **singles title** in the same week. Between matches, the sisters spent most of their time writing instant messages to each

Serena (left) and Venus (right) pose with their mom, Oracene, at the Lipton Championships in Florida in 1999.

other on-line. "I could swear I could hear Venus laughing [on-line],"[6] Serena later said. But Serena also began to see Venus as her biggest competition.

Sisterly Love

Venus and Serena tried not to play each other in competitions because they did not want to make each other lose. Although they could take turns playing the smaller events, some tournaments were too important to miss. At these times there was always a good chance they would have to play each other in the final match. This happened in March 1999 at the Lipton Championships in Key Biscayne, Florida.

All the top ten women's tennis champions were there, and the women's games were shown on prime-time television on Sunday. As usual, the sisters stayed together in the same hotel suite, and Venus drove Serena to the games in her black Porsche Carrera. They had also recently bought a piece of land together, and planned to build a mansion to share.

Throughout the match, most of the fans rooted for the Williams sisters, hoping to see them play each other in the finals. And the fans got their wish. The match between Venus and Serena was the first meeting of sisters in a pro women's tennis final since 1884. Tennis **commentator** Patrick McEnroe, who had played years before in a final against his own brother, John, said "It's pretty weird when the person on the other side of the net is family. It's a situation where you want to win but you don't want to win."[7]

The final match between the sisters was less intense and more full of errors than the games they had played against the other champions. Venus won, but she was not joyful as she walked to the net to hug Serena. But the sisters giggled together as they accepted their trophies. Venus put her arm around Serena as they walked off the court together, knowing they would probably face each other on the court again.

Serena

For a long time, Venus won every game she played against her sister, but Serena was moving up fast. In April 1999, Serena became the number nine player in the world. Venus was ranked number five. For the first time, both sisters were ranked in the top ten. At the French Open in June, they became the first sisters to win a **doubles** title in the twentieth century.

Venus and Serena both entered the U.S. Open in September 1999. Their father predicted that they would play each other in the finals. But Venus lost to number one Martina Hingis in the semifinals. Venus did not play her sister in the final match, as her father had predicted. Venus felt she had let down her family, friends, and fans by losing.

As she watched the final match from the stands, Venus wore black, and her face was somber, weary, and serious. Serena beat Hingis and became the first Williams sister to win the U.S. Open singles title. Venus tried to clap for her sister, but her hands barely touched. It was a historic victory, and Venus did not share in it.

Exhausted, Venus Williams wipes sweat from her face after being defeated by Martina Hingis in 1999.

After the game, Venus sat in the empty players lounge under Arthur Ashe Stadium until late into the night. She could barely speak. The loss was almost like a death for her. That night, she did not sleep. Venus doubted her abilities for the first time. Her mother said Serena had more love for the game, and her father said Serena would be the better player. Most tennis experts agreed that it would be Serena, not Venus, who would become the greatest tennis star.

Venus Rests

Things got worse for Venus when Serena beat her for the first time, on October 3, 1999, in Munich, Germany.

Career Highlights in the Life of Venus Williams

SINGLES VICTORIES

1998 — Grand Slam Cup, Oklahoma City, Miami

1999 — Hamburg, Italian Open, Miami, New Haven, Oklahoma City

2000 — New Haven, Olympics , San Diego, Stanford, U.S. Open

2001 — Hamburg, Miami, New Haven, San Diego, Wimbledon, U.S. Open

2002 — Amelia Island, Antwerp, Gold Coast, New Haven, Paris Indoors, San Diego, Stanford

DOUBLES VICTORIES

1998 — Oklahoma City (w/Serena), Zurich (w/Serena)

1999 — French Open (w/Serena), Hannover (w/Serena), U.S. Open (w/Serena)

2000 — Olympics (w/Serena), Wimbledon (w/Serena)

2001 — Australian Open (w/Serena)

2002 — Wimbledon (w/Serena)

ACCOMPLISHMENTS AND AWARDS

1992 — By the age of twelve, Venus held a 63-0 record in the U.S. Tennis Association section play in Southern California

1997 — First woman since 1978 to play in the U.S. Open Finals in her debut

1997 — First unseeded woman finalist at the U.S. Open since 1958

1997 — Received the Sanex World Tennis Association Tour Most Impressive Newcomer award

2000 — Won first Grand Slam singles title at Wimbledon; only the second African American to do so since Althea Gibson won thirty-two years earlier

2000 — Won second Grand Slam singles title at the U.S. Open

2000 — Named *Sports Illustrated* Women's Sportswoman of the Year

2000 — Venus and Serena are the only sisters in the twentieth century to have won a Grand Slam doubles title together

2001 — Voted Nasdaq Player of the Month four times

Venus stopped playing completely the next month, when her wrists began to ache. She said: "I couldn't type, I couldn't sew, I couldn't drive, at one point I couldn't hit a backhand. Every time I would try to hit a serve, my whole forearm would just spasm up. I was out of order."[8]

Venus had inflamed tendons, a condition known as tendinitis, in both her wrists. Because of the pain, she was forced to skip the Australian Open in January 2000 and the Ericsson Open in Florida in March. After months of silence from Venus, her father came to the Ericsson Open and announced that he was advising her to retire from tennis.

Venus read this news on the Internet, and said that she had no intention of retiring. But she had played only nine matches in 1999, and had not played at all in almost four months. Instead, she stayed home, watched tennis on television, and rested. She later said of the experience: "It was great. Serena and my mom would be gone on the tour, and me and Daddy were on the couch watching [TV] at midnight. I'd fall asleep and wake up disoriented, and my dad would put me into bed."[9]

After months of suffering through her doubt and pain, Venus began to heal. Then in the spring, she was rested and ready to get back in the game.

Chapter Four

Venus Number One

Venus got back into the game at the French Open in May 2000, after losing to her younger sister in 1999 and suffering through a painful bout of tendinitis. Venus was still weak at the French Open, so she built up her strength for the important tournament in Wimbledon, England, in July.

When the time came, Venus believed she was ready to win the important title. She was so confident, in fact, that she bought a ball gown to wear at the Champions' Ball before leaving her home in Florida. "I was scrambling around the mall, finding a dress. It was an extra incentive because if I didn't win, I wouldn't get to wear this wonderful dress. I picked it up the day we left."[10]

By the time Venus and Serena arrived at Wimbledon, the number one world champion Martina Hingis and the number two champ Lindsay Davenport had formed an alliance, saying they wanted to knock both sisters out of the game. But Venus was not shaken by such talk—and she was ready to win again.

Venus and Serena each won five games to qualify for the semifinals, when they would have to face each other. Serena had also bought a ball gown for the victory dance, and now she would have to play her sister for the chance to wear it.

Millennium Wimbledon Finals

When the two sisters finally faced each other in the semifinals at Wimbledon, Serena seemed nervous and

Venus defeated Serena in the semifinals at Wimbledon (pictured) in 2000.

Venus (right) comforts her sister after beating her at Wimbledon in 2000.

shaky on the court. Her game was described by sportswriters as sloppy and emotional. And Venus felt terrible taking the victory from her sister. At the end, Serena was in tears while Venus tried to comfort her.

For the first time, Venus admitted that winning was a bitter experience, and that she did not want the game to come between her and her sister. But ever since they were children, they knew they would have to face each other at important championship games. Venus said, "Our parents told us that this would happen. That's what we were working for. That's how we saw it."[11]

Venus went on to the final match, defeating **defending champion** Lindsay Davenport. Venus wore a special all-white dress tennis dress she designed herself. It had a scooped out back that showed her bare skin, and it was very daring for the conservative Wimbledon courts.

In addition to her cutting-edge fashion sense, Venus brought new life to the sport with her joyful post-game celebration. Immediately after winning her first Grand Slam victory, she laughed and leaped around in the grass. Later she was presented with a prize of $650,000 and the "Venus Rosewater Dish," a trophy given to each Wimbledon winner since 1866.

The next day, the tournament ended with the sisters capturing the women's doubles **crown**. It was the first time in history that two sisters have won the Wimbledon doubles titles. When asked about the trophy, Venus said the greatest joy was having her name engraved next to her sister's.

U.S. Open

In September, Venus beat Martina Hingis and Lindsay Davenport to win the U.S. Open. Venus had now beaten the top players in the world in the most important tournaments, proving she was the best player in women's tennis. After the last game, she skipped lightly to the net and twirled around, her face lit up with the happiness of her hard-won victories. She shook hands with Davenport, then trotted off to hug her family and dance for joy with her father. Serena, who had won the year before, praised her sister for doing a great job.

Olympic Gold and Beyond

Both sisters were chosen to represent the United States in the 2000 Summer Olympics that year in Syd-

As a symbol of their victory at the 2000 Olympics, Venus and Serena proudly wave U.S. flags.

ney, Australia. On September 20, Venus overpowered her Russian opponent to win the Olympic gold medal in the women's singles. She became the second player (after Steffi Graf in 1988) to win Wimbledon, the U.S. Open, and the Olympics all in the same year. Williams laughed when someone suggested that she had nothing left to achieve in tennis, saying, "I've never been world No. 1."[12]

The next day, Venus won another Olympic gold medal with Serena, taking the doubles match in just fifty minutes, the most one-sided final in Olympic tennis history. On that day, Venus became the first woman to win both the singles and doubles Olympic gold medals since Helen Wills in 1924.

Always the Best

On July 8, 2001, twenty-one-year-old Venus won her second Wimbledon championship in a row. The crowd had been rooting for her opponent, Justine Henin, until it became clear that Venus would win the match. But Venus was used to playing before crowds that were rooting for her opponent. "They wanted her to win. I've had a lot of experiences like that with the crowd. It's not often that I'm the player the crowd wants to win. For me, it's not important because I want to win. Who knows, there may be a day when they root for me."[13]

Despite the feelings of the crowds, Venus has always seen herself as the best player in the world. And that belief has helped her to achieve success, even when people did not recognize her talents. She said,

Venus cheerfully displays her Wimbledon trophy after winning in 2000.

"On paper I'm No. 2 but, in my mind, I'm always the best. I can't see anybody better than me. If I walk out on the court and think the next player is better, then I've already lost."[14]

A Champion

Although Venus had the desire to be number one in the world, she had not played as many games as her opponents because she put great importance on her study of fashion design. Though most considered her to be the best player in the world, she had never been given the title. In 2002 the system of ranking players was changed, however, and more points were given to those who won important tournaments such as Wimbledon.

On February 25, 2002, this change finally allowed Venus to take her rightful place as the very best player in the world. And Venus gave credit to her parents for making it possible. "Being No.1 was firstly my parents' dream, but it soon became mine too, so reaching it was great not only for me, but for them too."[15] Later she added, "I've enjoyed myself along the way, and I haven't limited myself just to playing tennis or made myself believe that was the only thing in life."[16]

From the time she was a little girl, Venus dreamed of being the greatest tennis player in the world, but she also placed great value on education and community service. While competing in one of the most physically demanding sports in the world, she took time to develop her mind as well as her backhand. In 2002 Venus Williams was the reigning tennis champion of the world. Whatever direction she decides to take with her life, there is little doubt that Venus Williams will always be a winner.

Notes

Chapter One: Tennis Lessons

1. Quoted in Kevin Chappell, "Richard Williams, Venus and Serena's Father Whips the Pros and Makes His Family No. 1 in Tennis," *Ebony*, June 2000, n.p.

Chapter Two: Young Professional

2. Quoted in "Venus and Serena Williams Timeline," *Sports Illustrated Online*, July 6, 2002. www.sportsillustrated.cnn.com.
3. Quoted in "Venus and Serena Williams Timeline."
4. Quoted in S.L. Price, "Venus Envy," *Sports Illustrated Online*, September 15, 1997. www.sportsillustrated.cnn.com.

Chapter Three: The Sisters

5. Quoted in "Davenport at the Door of the Greats," *Sunday Times—Sport*, September 13, 1998. www.sundaytimes.co.za.
6. Quoted in L. Jon Wertheim, "We Told You So," *Sports Illustrated Online*, April 5, 1999. www.sportsillustrated.cnn.com.
7. Quoted in Wertheim, "We Told You So."

8. Quoted in S.L. Price, "Simply Super," *Sports Illustrated For Women*, November/December 2000. www.sportsillustrated.cnn.com.

9. Quoted in S.L. Price, "For The Ages," *Sports Illustrated For Women*, July 17, 2000. www.sportsillustrated.cnn.com.

Chapter Four: Venus Number One

10. Quoted in "2000 Championship Interview with Venus Williams," July 8, 2000. www.champion ships.wimbledon.org.

11. Quoted in Associated Press, "Venus, Serena Williams Advance to Semifinals," *Shawnee News-Star*, May 2, 2000. www.news-star.com.

12. Quoted in "Venus and Serena Williams Timeline."

13. Quoted in Mike Donovan, "Venus Looks Forward to Future Success," July 8, 2001. www.wimbledon.org.

14. Quoted in Donovan, "Venus Looks Forward to Future Success."

15. Quoted in "Williams to Gain No. 1 Ranking for First Time," *ESPN.com*, February 19, 2002. www.espn.go.com.

16. Quoted in Teresa M. Walker, "Williams Happy She Did It Her Way," *The Detroit News*, February 24, 2002. www.detnews.com.

Glossary

commentator: A reporter or writer who comments on news events.

crown: A title, or championship, in a sport.

defending champion: One who has been the champion and must play an opponent to keep, or defend, the title.

doubles: A game with two players on each side.

endorse: To support; approval a celebrity gives to advertise a product.

Grand Slam: Tennis has four Grand Slam tournaments: the U.S. Open, the Australian Open, the French Open, and Wimbledon. These are the most important tournaments in the sport.

semifinals: A series of matches just before the final match in a tournament. The winners of the semifinal match plays the final match for a chance to win the tournament.

singles title: A championship match with one opponent on each side.

tournament: A series of contests in which a number of people compete. The one who wins the final round is the tournament winner. In tennis, a tournament consists of all the games played at a single event, such as Wimbledon or the U.S. Open.

For Further Exploration

Books

Gabriel Flynn, *Venus and Serena Williams (Sports Superstars)*. Chanhassen, MN: The Childs World, 2000. This biography is full of color photographs that show the emotions of the sisters on the tennis court. It tells the story of Venus's family and dreams as well as her tennis game.

Dave Rineberg, *Venus and Serena: My Seven Years as a Hitting Coach for the Williams*. Hollywood, FL: Frederick Fell, 2002. A unique close-up and personal look at the hard work, care, and commitment it took for the Williams sisters to rise to the very top of their sport.

A.R. Schaefer, *Venus and Serena Williams*. Mankato, MN: Capstone High-Interest Books, 2002. A short, easy-reading book about the lives and tennis careers of Venus and Serena.

Elizabeth Sirimarco, *Tennis*. Vero Beach, FL: Rourke Corporation, 1994. A book for young people about the game of tennis.

Websites

Sisterfriends.com (www.sisterfriends.com). A website with a chat room for women of color, featuring Venus and Serena Williams.

Venus and Serena Williams Dreams Coming True (www.VenusandSerena.homestead.com). A fan-based website on Venus and Serena Williams. Includes pictures, links, biography, new information, and a message board.

VenusSerenaFans.com (www.venusserenafans.com). The website includes extensive information on the sisters, including current news and results.

Index

Picture Credits

Cover Photo: © Reuters NewMedia Inc./CORBIS

© Associated Press, AP, 25, 34

© Al Bello/Getty Images, 22, 26

© Clive Brunskill/Getty Images, 29

© Patrick J. Forden/CORBIS SYGMA, 14

© Jason Hawkes/CORBIS, 33

© Mike Hewett/Getty Images, 5

© Hulton/Archive by Getty Images, 20, 21

© Ken Levine/Getty Images, 6, 8, 12, 16

© Alex Livesey/Getty Images, 38

© Gary M. Prior/Getty Images, 18, 36

© Reuters NewMedia Inc./CORBIS, 10

About
the Authors

P.M. Boekhoff is an author of twenty nonfiction books for children. She has written about early American history, science, and the lives of creative people. In addition, Boekhoff is an artist who has created murals and theatrical scenics and illustrated many book covers. In her spare time, she paints, draws, writes poetry, and studies herbal medicine.

Stuart A. Kallen is the author of more than 150 nonfiction books for children and young adults. He has written extensively about Native Americans and American history. In addition, Mr. Kallen has written award-winning children's videos and television scripts. In his spare time, Kallen is a singer/songwriter/guitarist in San Diego, California.